OUR VIOLENT EARTH

VOLCANOES

Fiona Waters

OUR VIOLENT EARTH

VOLCANOES

Other titles in this series:
EARTHQUAKES • FLOODS • STORMS

Cover photograph: The Arenal volcano exploding in Costa Rica.

Title page: A scientist working at Krafla in Iceland.

Contents page: Red-hot lava flows into the Pacific Ocean off Hawaii.

This book is a simplified version of the title 'Volcanoes' in Hodder Wayland's 'Restless Planet' series.

Language level consultant: Norah Granger
Editor: Belinda Hollyer   Designer: Jane Hawkins

Text copyright © 2001 Hodder Wayland
Volume copyright © 2001 Hodder Wayland

First published in 2001 by Hodder Wayland,
an imprint of Hodder Children's Books.

British Library Cataloguing in Publication Data
Waters, Fiona
Volcanoes. - (Our violent earth)
1. Volcanoes - Juvenile literature
I.Title
551.2'1
ISBN 0 7502 3512 8

Printed and bound in Italy by
G. Canale & C.S.p.A., Turin

Hodder Children's Books
A division of Hodder Headline Ltd
338 Euston Road, London NW1 3BH

Acknowledgements
The publishers would like to thank the following for allowing their photographs to be reproduced in this book: Bruce Coleman *Contents page*/Pacific Stock, 6/Orion Service & Trading Co Inc., 16/C.C. Lockwood, 19/Pacific Stock, 33/Derek Croucher, 36/Stephen Bond, 40/Dr Sandro Prato; DERA/Still Pictures 32; ET Archive/National Gallery 22; Mary Evans 29; GeoScience Features 7, 21, 42, 43; Michael Holford 28; Image Bank 45 (bottom)/Guido A. Rossi; Impact 24/Andy Johnstone; Michael Holford 28; NASA GSFC/Science Photo Library 21; Oxford Scientific Films 35/Norbert Rosing, 39 (bottom)/Richard Packwood; Photri 37/Mark E. Gibson; Planet Earth *Title page*/I. & V. Krafft, 11 (top)/Krafft, 14/Annie Price, 15/Krafft, 18/V. & I. Bourseiller, 31/William M. Smithey Jr, 34/Frank Krahmer, 39 (top)/I. & V. Krafft, 41/Annie Price, 44-5/I. & V. Krafft; Popperfoto 27/Colin Braley/Reuters; Frank Spooner/Gamma 4-5/Alain Buu, 20/Bouvet, Hires & Duclos; Tony Stone /Schafer & Hill *cover*; Wayland Picture Library 5 (top).

Illustrations: Peter Bull 8; Nick Hawken 9, 20; Tim Mayer 7, 10, 12, 13, 14, 15, 17, 25, 30, 31, 37, 38; Malcolm Walker 35, 43.

Contents

Introducing Volcanoes

In 1997 the Soufrière Hills volcano in Montserrat erupted. The island was very badly damaged, and many people had to leave their homes for ever. ▼

When a volcano erupts it is one of the most amazing sights in the world. It is also very dangerous. A volcano can blow poisonous gases and tonnes of dust high into the atmosphere. It can cover the land round about with hot lava and ash. It will also damage roads and bring down telephone lines. Sometimes many people are killed by a volcano.

 The damage on the island of Martinique after the eruption of Mont Pelée in 1902.

66 *EYEWITNESS* 99

"As we reached St Pierre we could see red flames pouring up into the sky from the mountain. Great clouds of black smoke hung over the volcano. There was a huge explosion at about 7.45 a.m. The mountain was blown to pieces. The side of the volcano fell down and a great wall of flames rushed towards us. The flames flowed down to the harbour where the ships were moored. When the fire hit the sea, the water boiled and steam rose into the air. The harbour had been crowded with people, but after the explosion no-one was left alive."

A report of the eruption of Mont Pelée on the island of Martinique in 1902. It was written by an officer from one of the ships in the harbour.

What is a volcano?

A volcano is really just a hole in the earth's surface that liquid rock, gas and dust escape through. Volcanoes can be different sizes and shapes. There are volcanoes erupting all the time, but we only hear about the very big ones. Eruptions cause a lot of damage and can kill thousands of people. They can change the landscape completely. But they can also make new land as well.

How many volcanoes are there?

There are about 550 active volcanoes in the world. Each year about 50 of these will erupt, but only a few cause great damage.

Not all volcanoes are still active. Some, like Mount Kilimanjaro in Kenya, have not erupted for thousands of years. These are called extinct volcanoes. Others have been quiet for a long time. These are called sleeping, or dormant, volcanoes. They can suddenly erupt again, like Mount Fuji in Japan. It last erupted in 1707, but it could erupt again at any time.

There are also many volcanoes at the bottom of the seas and oceans. These bubble away under the water where they cannot be seen.

DID YOU KNOW?

Over 80 per cent of the Earth's surface was once volcanic. Volcanoes have changed the way the Earth was formed, and they have made new rock.

▼ Japan's Mount Fuji is a dormant volcano.

▲ The red dots on this map show the location of volcanoes around the world.

Where are volcanoes found?

Volcanoes are found mostly on the edge of the big continents, as you can see on the map above. Others form chains of islands, or long lines of mountains underwater. More than half the active volcanoes in the world above sea-level are found round the Pacific Ocean. They are known as the 'Ring of Fire'.

These jets of water are called 'black smokers'. They bubble up from the ocean bed wherever there are active underwater volcanoes. ▶

What Causes Volcanoes?

The Earth has three main layers. These are the crust, the mantle and the core. The crust is thetop layer. It is made of solid rock and is not the same thickness everywhere. For example, it is more than 60 kilometres thick under mountains. But it is only 5 kilometres thick under the oceans. The mantle is a thick layer of molten rock, called magma. The core has an outer layer of liquid and a solid centre.

The temperature inside the Earth's core is more than 5,000 degrees Celsius. This means the Earth is a huge fiery ball of hot molten rock inside the crust of cool hard rock.

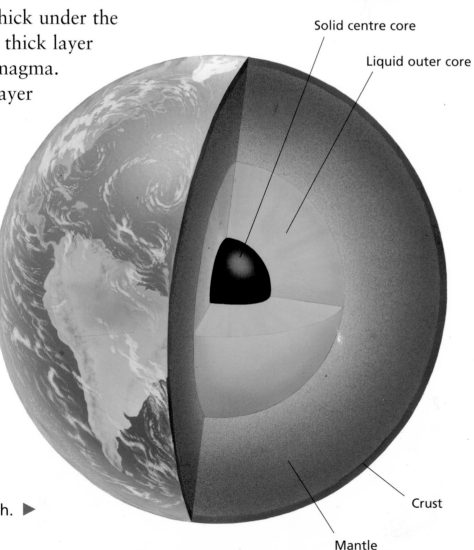

Solid centre core

Liquid outer core

Crust

Mantle

The main layers of the Earth. ▶

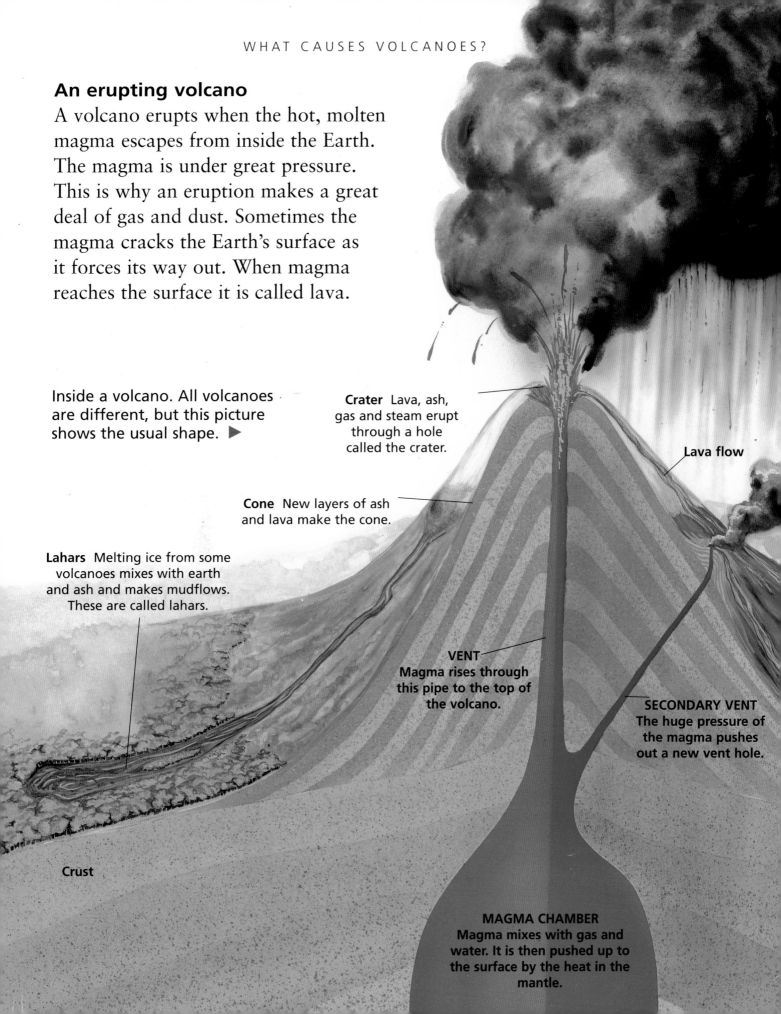

An erupting volcano

A volcano erupts when the hot, molten magma escapes from inside the Earth. The magma is under great pressure. This is why an eruption makes a great deal of gas and dust. Sometimes the magma cracks the Earth's surface as it forces its way out. When magma reaches the surface it is called lava.

Inside a volcano. All volcanoes are different, but this picture shows the usual shape. ▶

Crater Lava, ash, gas and steam erupt through a hole called the crater.

Lava flow

Cone New layers of ash and lava make the cone.

Lahars Melting ice from some volcanoes mixes with earth and ash and makes mudflows. These are called lahars.

VENT Magma rises through this pipe to the top of the volcano.

SECONDARY VENT The huge pressure of the magma pushes out a new vent hole.

Crust

MAGMA CHAMBER Magma mixes with gas and water. It is then pushed up to the surface by the heat in the mantle.

Volcanoes and Plates

The Earth's crust is its thinnest layer. It is broken up into large pieces, called tectonic plates. Each plate contains some land and some seabed. Huge currents of magma circulate deep in the mantle. This makes the plates move about very slowly on the Earth's surface.

DID YOU KNOW?

The word 'volcano' comes from the name of an island called Vulcano, in the Mediterranean Sea. Thousands of years ago, people thought the lava erupting from Vulcano came from Vulcan's forge. Vulcan was a blacksmith, and one of the Roman gods.

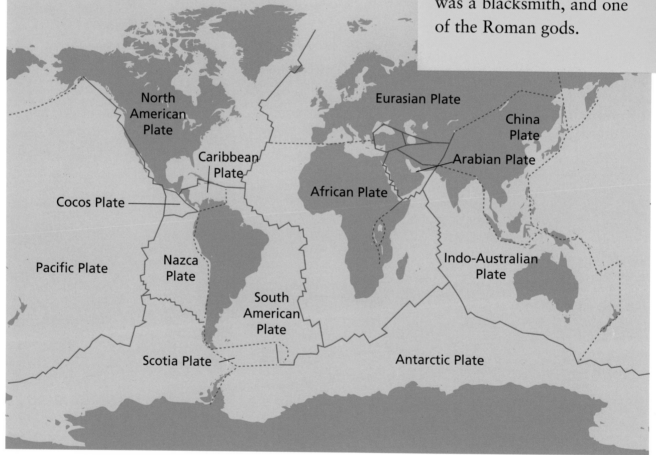

Look at the map on page 7, and the one on this page. You will see that many of the world's volcanoes are along the edges of the plates. New rock is often being made and destroyed along the edges of the plates. So most eruptions and earthquakes happen here.

▲ This map shows the edges of the Earth's tectonic plates. Most eruptions and earthquakes happen in these areas.

The Pacific 'Ring of Fire'

More than half of all the volcanoes in the world are found in the Pacific 'Ring of Fire'. This 'Ring of Fire' makes a big circle round the Pacific Ocean. Many of the volcanoes are very famous. One, called Cotopaxi, is in Ecuador, in South America and erupted in 1928. Another is Mount St Helens in the USA, which erupted in 1980.

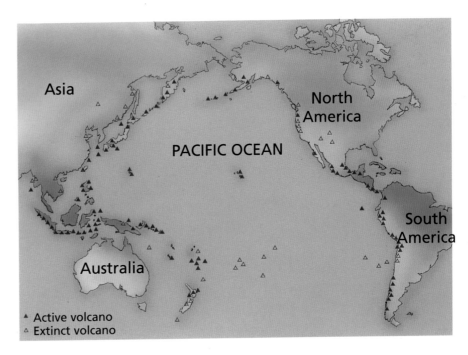

▲ This map shows the volcanoes in the Pacific 'Ring of Fire'.

Spreading centres

The edge of some of the plates is along a line on the surface of the land. For example, one side of the Pacific Plate is along the coast of America. The edges of others are at the bottom of the ocean. There are enormous ranges of mountains and volcanoes hidden at the bottom of the sea. Underwater volcanoes are making new rock all the time as the lava pours out.

The Cotopaxi volcano is 5900 metres above sea-level. It is the world's highest active volcano. ▼

Types of volcano

There are three main types of volcano. Scientists decide what type a volcano is by finding out how it has been formed.

1. Subduction volcanoes

A subduction volcano is made when plates move towards each other and then collide. The place where the two pieces of crust meet is called the subduction zone.

The heavier plate is forced under the other into the mantle, where it heats up and melts. This melted material is pushed back to the surface of the Earth. It is under great pressure, and often erupts explosively.

These diagrams show how subduction volcanoes are formed. ▼

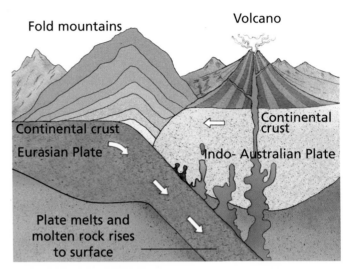

▲ **2. Continent to continent margins**
Two land plates, the Indo-Australian Plate and the Eurasian Plate, have collided in Northern India. The melting crust is pushed down into the mantle by the collision. This causes the volcano to erupt.

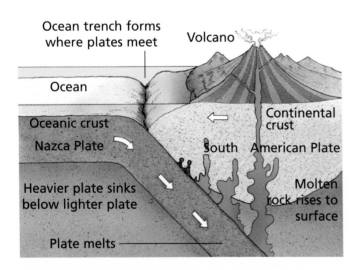

▲ **1. Ocean to continent margins**
Along the west coast of South America, the Nazca Plate and the South American plate have collided. The Nazca Plate is heavier and sinks below the lighter South American plate. This causes volcanic eruptions in the Andes mountains.

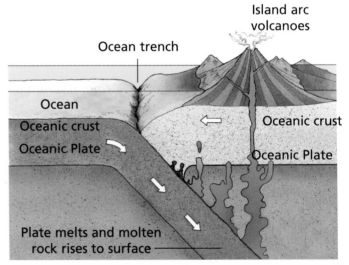

▲ **3. Ocean to ocean margins**
Sometimes two plates meet under the ocean. The heavier plate slides under the lighter one. When the magma rises to the surface, it makes a chain of volcanoes called an island arc. The islands of Japan are an island arc.

2. Rift volcanoes

When plates move apart, magma rises through the gap between the plates and creates new rock. The new volcanoes are called rift volcanoes.

There are more rift volcanoes than subduction volcanoes. We do not hear much about them as most of them are hidden under the sea. They erupt more gently than other kinds of volcano.

Iceland is one of the few places where rift volcanoes are found on land.

3. Hot-spot volcanoes

Some volcanoes erupt away from the edges of the plates. They are formed when rising magma forces its way to the surface. It comes from deep within the mantle – a 'hot spot'. When the plate moves, the old volcano is carried away from the hot spot and becomes extinct. When the pressure builds up next time, the new magma makes a new volcano.

There are many 'hot-spot' volcanoes in the Hawaiian Islands.

How rift volcanoes are formed ▼

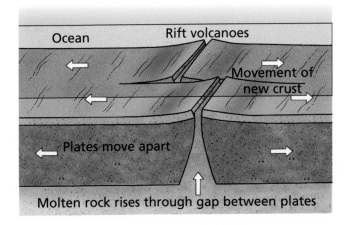

How 'hot-spot' volcanoes are formed ▼

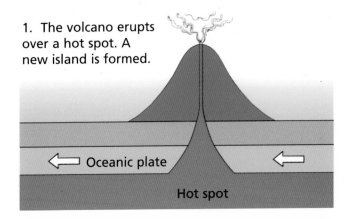

1. The volcano erupts over a hot spot. A new island is formed.

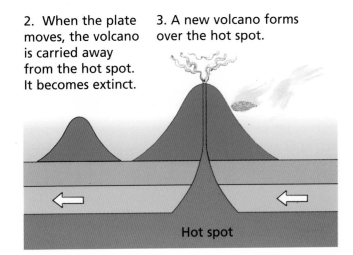

2. When the plate moves, the volcano is carried away from the hot spot. It becomes extinct.

3. A new volcano forms over the hot spot.

Volcanoes can be different shapes and sizes. The shape and size depend on:

- the kind of eruption
- the kind of lava made in the eruption
- how much lava and ash pile up to make the volcano.

There are four main kinds of volcano.

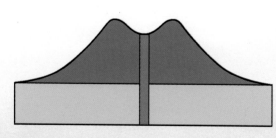

▲ An ash and cinder cone volcano

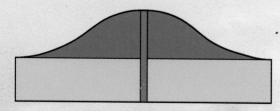

▲ An acid lava cone volcano

▼ Mount Ngauruhoe in New Zealand is an acid lava cone volcano.

1. Ash and cinder cone volcanoes

These are formed when small, solid bits of ash and rock are flung up in the eruption. They have steep sides but are not very tall. Paricutin in Mexico is an ash and cinder cone volcano.

2. Acid lava cone volcanoes

These are formed when the lava is very thick. It moves slowly, like treacle. These volcanoes have steep sides.

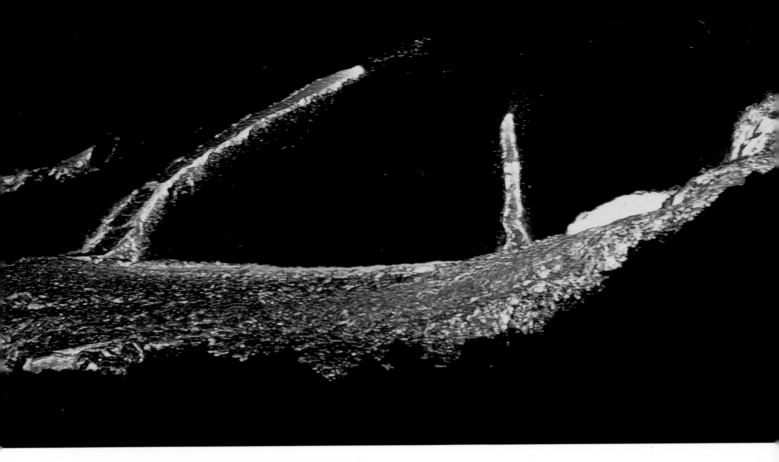

▲ This lava flow has made a shield volcano.

3. Shield volcanoes

Shield volcanoes are very big and have very gently sloping sides. They are mostly made up of lava with very little ash. The lava is very thin and runny. It spreads a long way. Mauna Loa in Hawaii is a shield volcano.

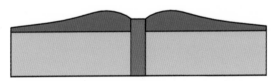

▲ A shield volcano

4. Composite cone volcanoes

Composite cone volcanoes are the most common volcanoes. They are usually quite tall. They are made when a quiet eruption of runny lava is followed by an eruption of thick lava. Composite cone volcanoes have more ash than shield volcanoes. This makes their sides very steep. Mount Fuji in Japan is a composite cone volcano.

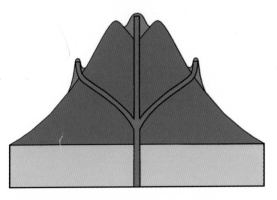

▲ A composite cone volcano

Volcanic eruptions

When the lava is thin and runny, it flows easily from the volcano. An eruption like this is usually quite gentle. But when the lava is thick, the volcano erupts with an explosion. Thick lava cools down quickly too, and it may form a solid plug inside the main vent of the volcano.

Calderas

When the vent of a volcano is blocked, pressure builds up. After a while, the pressure is so great that there is an explosion which blows the top off the volcano. The explosion makes a large crater which is called a caldera. This crater will fill up with water if the volcano becomes inactive, and a lake is made. The world's largest caldera is 22 kilometres long, and about 16 kilometres wide.

This is Crater Lake at the top of Mount Mazama in Oregon, in the USA. ▼

Different kinds of volcanic eruption

There are different kinds of volcanic eruption. The gentlest is called a Hawaiian eruption. These make shield volcanoes. The most violent are called Plinian eruptions. In a Plinian eruption, the cone of the volcano collapses and makes a crater. Plinian eruptions are named after a Roman teacher called Pliny the Elder. He was killed in AD 79 when Mount Vesuvius erupted.

❝ EYEWITNESS ❞

"The earth had been shaking for days. When night came, tall flames leapt up from many places on Mount Vesuvius. Then the sea was sucked back from the shore. We saw many sea creatures left behind on the sand. A great black cloud rose up, filled with long tongues of flame. Ash was falling. Many people prayed to the gods. But most people believed it was the end of the world."

Part of a letter from Pliny the Younger describing the eruption of Vesuvius in AD 79.

Hawaiian The most gentle eruptions. The lava is runny and makes a volcano with gentle slopes. ▶

Strombolian Gentle but fairly regular eruptions. The lava is sticky and gas, ash and cinders erupt. ▶

◀ **Vulcanian** The eruptions are violent, and the lava is very thick.

Peléean The eruptions are violent. The lava is thick and sticky, and there is a cloud of ash, and pumice. ▼

Plinian The most violent eruptions. Cinders, gas and ash are hurled high into the sky. The cone of the volcano often collapses to make a crater. ▶

Volcanic Hazards

There are many hazards or dangers when a volcano erupts. Red-hot lava is one but there are many others. These hazards can harm people and the land around the volcano. There are direct or primary hazards, and indirect or secondary hazards.

Primary hazards

The main hazards after a volcanic explosion are ash, dust, lava and poisonous gases.

Ash and dust

When a volcano explodes, old lava is blasted into tiny pieces. It is thrown high into the air with dust and ash. This can be fine dust or the size of small pebbles. The pieces can even be as big as 25 centimetres across. These big bombs of lava are called tephra.

▲ After an eruption, a farmer tries to move his pig to safety.

This diagram shows the different kinds of volcanic hazard. ▼

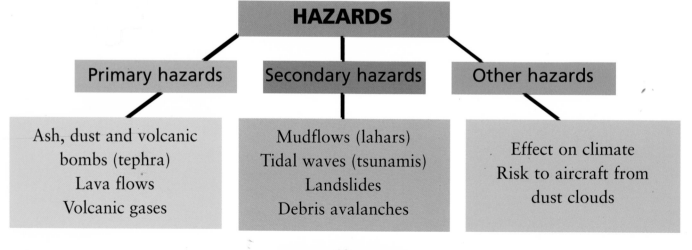

HAZARDS

Primary hazards	Secondary hazards	Other hazards
Ash, dust and volcanic bombs (tephra) Lava flows Volcanic gases	Mudflows (lahars) Tidal waves (tsunamis) Landslides Debris avalanches	Effect on climate Risk to aircraft from dust clouds

Often, tephra is spread over a wide area. Tephra can damage buildings and make roofs collapse. Ash and dust in the air make it difficult for people to breathe. It can clog up machines. Good farming land can be buried. When Vesuvius erupted, the ancient city of Pompeii was buried under 6 metres of ash.

Sometimes the hot ash flows down the side of the volcano like an avalanche. It can reach a speed of up to 300 kilometres an hour, and it burns everything in its path.

Lava

Lava usually moves very slowly, only a few centimetres an hour. But sometimes it moves much faster. In 1986 about 300 hundred people in the Congo were killed by lava moving at more than 30 kilometres an hour.

Volcanic gases

Magma contains many nasty-smelling gases which go into the atmosphere when a volcano erupts. Scientists believe that Popocatépetl near Mexico City sends 8,000 tonnes of sulphur dioxide gas into the atmosphere each day.

▲ Red-hot lava flows into the Pacific Ocean near Hawai'i, making huge explosions.

NEWS REPORT

Villagers in the African country of Cameroon are to be moved to safety on Monday. The Mount Cameroon volcano began erupting last week. Lava is flowing near homes and businesses. Gas masks have been given out to protect people from gas and dust. President Biya arrived by helicopter yesterday to look at the damage.

Adapted from a Reuters report, April 1999

Secondary hazards

A volcanic eruption can bring other less direct dangers, or secondary hazards. These can be mudflows called lahars, avalanches, and tidal waves which are called tsunamis.

Lahars

When ash and dust move down the sides of a volcano, they mix with water to make a mudflow. The mudflow gets faster as it moves downhill and picks up rocks as it goes. In 1985 the Nevado del Ruiz volcano exploded high in the Andes mountains. A cloud of hot gas melted the snow around it. With mud and ash it made a lahar 40 metres deep. This rushed downhill at 50 kilometres an hour and buried the nearby town of Armero in 8 metres of mud. Over 20,000 people were killed.

▲ A man sits in the wreckage of his home in Armero in Colombia.

This diagram shows how the town of Armero was buried by the lahar. ▼

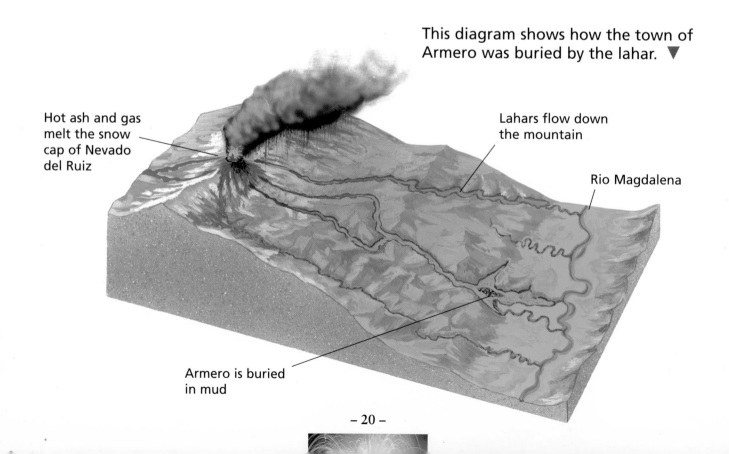

Hot ash and gas melt the snow cap of Nevado del Ruiz

Lahars flow down the mountain

Rio Magdalena

Armero is buried in mud

Landslides and debris avalanches

There are often small earthquakes at the same time as a volcanic eruption. These can cause landslides or avalanches of rock. This is what happened when Mount St Helens volcano in the USA collapsed during its eruption in 1980.

Tsunamis

Some big volcanic eruptions cause huge tidal waves which are called tsunamis. These tidal waves can be caused by underwater eruptions too. Underwater eruptions push great masses of gas into the water. This stirs up the water and makes great tidal waves.

An avalanche of rock pours down the side of Mount St Helens. ▼

Other effects

A volcanic eruption can have effects far away from the volcano itself.

Black skies and fiery sunsets are often seen right after an eruption. This is because dust can hang in the air a long way from the volcano. Some scientists think that the dinosaurs died out because a dust cloud from a volcano hid the sun. Many plants died because it was colder and so the plant-eating dinosaurs died. Then the dinosaurs that fed on them died too.

This painting, called *The Fighting Temeraire*, is by the English artist Joseph Turner. The volcano Tambora, in Indonesia, erupted in 1815. Afterwards there were dust-filled sunsets. Joseph Turner may have painted the sky in his picture to look like those sunsets. ▼

Spreading dust clouds

We still don't know how much volcanoes change our climate. In 1815, world temperatures fell by 1.1 degrees Celsius after the eruption of Tambora in Indonesia. The next year was called 'the year without a summer'. In the north-east of the USA, heavy snow fell when it should have been summer.

▲ This satellite image was recorded in 1986, after Mount Louise in South America had erupted. The red shows how much ash and dust were in the atmosphere.

When the dust from a volcanic eruption is blown high into the atmosphere, the wind sends it far around the world. We know this from information collected from satellites. Volcanic dust can stay in the atmosphere for many years.

NEWS REPORT

A pilot flying above the Aleutian Islands in Alaska saw the latest eruption of the Shishaldin volcano. A cloud of ash and steam rose 9 kilometres into the atmosphere. The eruption is a danger to aircraft. Flights to Ulalaska and Dutch Harbour have been cancelled.

Adapted from Reuters report, April 20 1999

In 1990 a plane flew close to the Redoubt volcano in Alaska, in the USA, when it was erupting. Ash from the volcano stalled all four engines of the plane. It fell more than 3,900 metres before the pilot was able to save it from crashing.

Volcanic Disasters

▲ A cloud of ash and dust pours from the Chances Peak volcano in 1995.

Montserrat

In July 1995, people on the tiny island of Montserrat in the Caribbean woke up to a strong smell of sulphur. No one knew where it was coming from. But then experts decided it was coming from the Chances Peak volcano in the south of the island. The volcano had not erupted for 400 years, but now it was coming to life.

Why did the volcano erupt?

Two tectonic plates met about 300 kilometres from the island. The heavier plate was pushed into the mantle, and then melted. The molten magma was pushed up through the crust. It exploded at the top of Chances Peak.

> ## 66 EYEWITNESS 99
>
> *"People were getting worried. Those living near the volcano were moved to a safer part of the island. Then steam and mudflows came from the volcano,"* said Doris Francis, a local teacher.
>
> A report from the *Newcastle Journal* in November 1997

MONTSERRAT VOLCANO DIARY

1995
18 July *Small earthquakes, tephra falls. Steam explosions suggest there will be an eruption soon.*

Mid-August *6,000 people are evacuated (moved) to the northern end of the island.*

21 August *Largest eruption so far. Ash and dust fall on the capital, Plymouth, making it dark for 30 minutes.*

December *People are evacuated from Plymouth for the first time. There are several small ash eruptions.*

1996
April *There are more severe eruptions. Very hot gas, ash, rock and dust are thrown 12 kilometres up into the air, and then down the side of the mountain. (This is called a pyroclastic flow.) People are moved out of the danger areas again.*

1997
January *Ash and grit fall over all the island. Great damage to land and buildings. Pyroclastic flows rush down the sides of the volcano at 200 kilometres an hour.*

25 June *The peak of the volcano collapses. Pyroclastic flows cover almost 4 square kilometres. Ash reaches 9 kilometres into the air, hiding the sun for 20 minutes.*

27 June *Four people are buried by the ash and rubble.*

August *Plymouth is destroyed. Ash falls are seen 40 kilometres away on the island of Antigua.*

1998
Volcanic activity reported during the year...

1999
13 January *An eruption sends an avalanche of hot gases and rocks down the side of the volcano. Ash is thrown 6 kilometres into the air.*

Montserrat

The island was divided into areas. People were allowed to stay in the safer areas. ▼

N

0 km 2
0 mile 1

St John's

MONTSERRAT

Airport

Salem
Montserrat Volcano Observatory

Spanish Point ●

Soufrière Hills

New Dome

Plymouth

St Patrick's

South Soufrière Hill

Hazard areas (April 1997)

No entry

Entry for essential visitors only

Prepare for possible evacuation

Full occupation (possible evacuation)

Full occupation

NEWS REPORT

Yesterday, people in part of the island of Montserrat were ordered to be evacuated at night. There is a growing danger from a volcanic eruption.

The Governor of Montserrat said people on the south coast should move to the north by 6pm. They could return to work during the day.

The order followed an eruption from Chance's Peak volcano on Monday afternoon.

About 5,000 people were ordered to move to the north of the island where they are thought to be safe from the volcano.

The island was calm yesterday. Many people had returned to help clean up the volcanic dust.

Adapted from a report in
The Daily Telegraph on 23 August 1995

The effect of the Chance's Peak eruption

The island of Montserrat has been badly affected by volcanic activity. Twenty people have died. The south of the island is deserted and uninhabitable. Many islanders have been evacuated. Some, like Doris Francis, have left the island for ever. In three years, the island's population has gone from over 11,000 to just 4,000. The capital, Plymouth, and the airport have been abandoned. Seven villages have been completely destroyed.

▲ Newspapers reported the eruption and evacuation plans.

66 EYEWITNESS 99

"We moved to a safe area in the north in August 1995. We came home after a few weeks, but in December we had to go back to the north. I was teaching in a tent. In June 1997 a huge flow of lava flowed from the volcano. The capital, Plymouth, was covered in ash. We decided it was time to leave."

Doris Francis and her family left their home in Montserrat in November 1997. They now live in the north of England. This report is from the *Newcastle Journal*, November 1997.

Helping the victims

Montserrat is an island that belongs to Britain. By 1999, the British government had given £59 million in aid to help the island cope with the disaster. Temporary shelters were put up for people who had lost their homes. Those who wanted to emigrate to Britain were told they would be given money to help them.

In 1995, the Montserrat Volcano Observatory was built about 6 kilometres from the volcano. Helicopters fly over the volcano every day. People will be given early warning of any future eruptions.

Plymouth, the capital of Montserrat, was buried under ash and dust from the volcano. ▼

Major eruptions in history

The Montserrat eruption is only one of the many eruptions to make headlines around the world. Some eruptions in history caused so much damage they are still famous today.

Vesuvius, Italy

The most famous eruption ever was Mount Vesuvius. In AD 79, it suddenly erupted after being dormant for centuries. A massive explosion blew away the whole top of the mountain. An enormous cloud of gas and hot ash was blown towards the towns of Pompeii and Herculaneum. Tonnes of ash fell on the towns for more than two days. When the rain fell, the ash turned to concrete. Everything was preserved just as it was when the volcano exploded. In the seventeenth century, archaeologists began to uncover the remains.

DID YOU KNOW?

Scientists think the biggest eruption ever took place 2.2 million years ago. It happened in what is now called Yellowstone National Park in the USA.

◄ The remains of the Roman town of Pompeii. You can see Mount Vesuvius in the distance.

Major volcanic eruptions

Yellowstone, USA	2.2 million years BC	2,500 cubic km ash produced
Santorini, Greece	1550 BC	Island destroyed
Vesuvius, Italy	AD 79	Approx. 20,000 dead and town of Pompeii buried under ash
Etna, Italy	1669	20,000 dead
Tambora, Indonesia	1815	92,000 dead
Krakatoa, Indonesia	1883	36,000 dead
Mont Pelée, Martinique	1902	26,000 dead
Novarupta, Alaska, USA	1912	20 cubic km material erupted
Mount St Helens, USA	1980	66 dead
Nevado del Ruiz, Colombia	1984	22,000 dead
Mount Pinatubo, Philippines	1991	420 dead

Krakatoa, Indonesia

In May 1883, a volcano erupted on the island of Krakatoa in Indonesia. Then on 27 August, there were four giant explosions. One was the loudest ever recorded. People who were 4,000 kilometres away said they heard it. The explosion blew the tiny island to bits.

Ash and dust rose 80 kilometres into the air, and huge tidal waves 36 metres high were produced. There were red sunsets for over a year because of the dust. The blast was the same force as if 200 megatonnes of dynamite had been set off. Hundreds of nearby coastal villages were flooded, and 36,000 people were killed.

▲ This nineteenth-century picture shows a ship sailing through the sea near Krakatoa. The sea is full of bodies, the day after the eruption.

Mount St Helens

Until it erupted in 1980, Mount St Helens was the fifth-highest mountain in Washington State, in the USA.

Early in May 1980, there were small earth tremors in the area around Mount St Helens. A bulge on the summit could be seen. Then, at 8.32 a.m. on 18 May, there was a violent explosion. Part of the mountain broke loose.

A hot, thick cloud of ash and gas slid down the side of the mountain. Trees 28 kilometres away were burnt, and 66 people were killed.

The volcano rumbled on for nine hours after the explosion. Just three days after the explosion, dust was found in cities 4,000 kilometres away.

 DID YOU KNOW?
The largest eruption in the twentieth century was at Novarupta in Alaska. In 1912, more than 20 cubic kilometres of magma erupted in five days. This was 30 times as much as Mount St Helens in 1980.

This diagram shows why Mount St Helens erupted. ▼

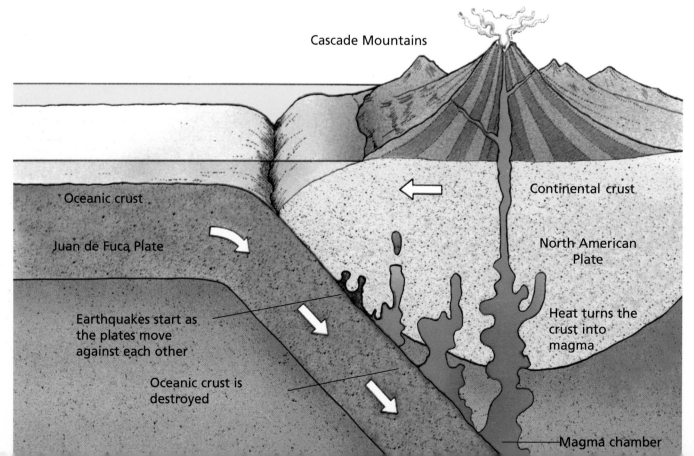

Mount St Helens

Cascade Mountains

Oceanic crust

Juan de Fuca Plate

Earthquakes start as the plates move against each other

Oceanic crust is destroyed

Continental crust

North American Plate

Heat turns the crust into magma

Magma chamber

The eruption of Mount St Helens caused huge damage over a big area. ▼

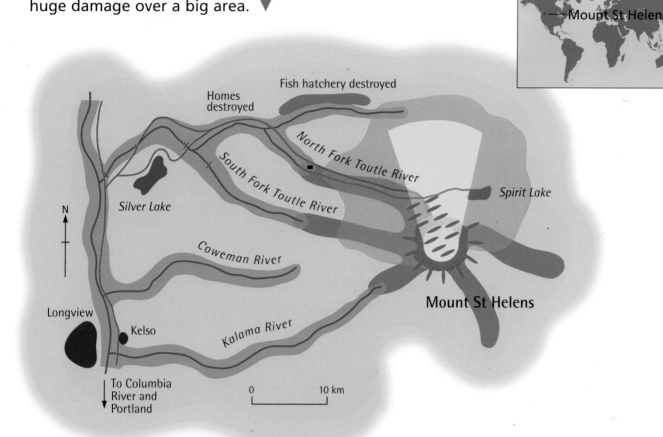

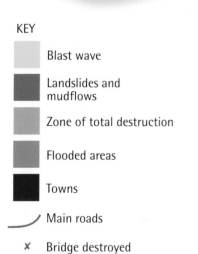

KEY

▢	Blast wave
▢	Landslides and mudflows
▢	Zone of total destruction
▢	Flooded areas
▢	Towns
╱	Main roads
✗	Bridge destroyed
◞	Volcanic bombs and ash

The eruption blew the cone of Mount St Helens apart. You can see the remains of some trees at the bottom of the photograph. ▶

Volcanic Landscapes

A volcanic eruption can change the landscape in a few seconds. When a volcano erupts, homes and trees are destroyed. Rivers change course, and the surface of the land changes as the lava flows become hard.

Igneous rocks

Much of the Earth's crust is igneous, which means 'made by fire'. Igneous rocks are made when molten material, like lava, cools and hardens on the Earth's surface.

There are many different kinds of igneous rock. Dark, runny lava is called basalt when it hardens. Basalt is the most common volcanic rock. Thick lava moves more slowly and can form pumice or a volcanic glass called obsidian. The best known igneous rock formed below the Earth's surface is granite. It is found in mountainous areas.

▲ You can see the volcano Vesuvius in Italy on this satellite photograph. It stands out clearly from the land around it.

The basalt columns of the Giants Causeway in Northern Ireland were formed 12 million years ago as a lava flow cooled quickly. ▶

Other volcanic landforms

The red-hot magma in the Earth's crust can make other landforms as well as volcanoes. When the magma heats water underground, it can make hot springs and geysers.

▲ These hot springs are at Lake Bogoria in Kenya.

Hot springs

Hot springs are found in many places around the world. Hot magma moves upwards quite close to the Earth's surface. Rainwater falls down through the rocks and meets the hot magma. The magma heats the water which then goes back to the surface as a hot spring. There are many hot springs in active volcanic areas like Iceland, Japan and New Zealand. They are also found in dormant volcanic areas like the Yellowstone National Park in the USA.

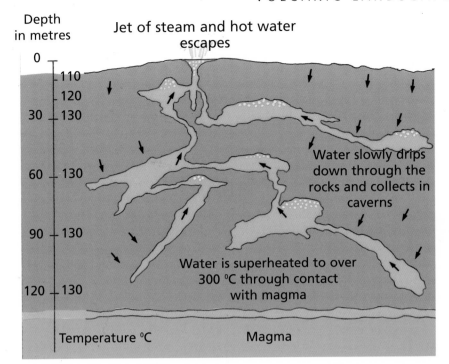

Depth in metres

Jet of steam and hot water escapes

0
110
120
30 — 130
60 — 130
90 — 130
120 — 130

Water slowly drips down through the rocks and collects in caverns

Water is superheated to over 300 °C through contact with magma

Temperature °C   Magma

▲ This diagram shows how a geyser is formed.

Geysers

Water that is very deep underground can be 'superheated' to temperatures of more than 300 degrees Celsius. It is so hot that it makes steam which expands in explosions. When it reaches the surface, a jet of hot air and steam is flung high into the air. This is called a geyser.

Geysers are usually found in areas which still have active volcanoes. Iceland has about 30 active geysers. There are more than 100 small geysers on the Kamchatka Peninsula in Russia. But there are over 200 in Yellowstone National Park. Some geysers erupt often. 'Old Faithful' in Yellowstone National Park shoots into the air every 30 to 90 minutes. The largest active geyser in the world is Steamboat Geyser in Yellowstone National Park. It sends steam and water more than 90 metres into the air.

The Castle Geyser in Yellowstone National Park, in the USA. ▼

Underground activity

Most magma hardens while it is still underground. Many different landforms can only be seen when the rock above them is worn away, or when there is an earthquake or volcanic eruption.

Batholiths

Batholiths are large, uneven masses of molten rock which harden within the crust. One of the largest in North America is the Coast Range batholith in Alaska and western Canada. In the UK, one of the largest granite batholiths is Dartmoor in south-west England. The rocks above it have worn away, so it can now be seen.

Volcanic rocks which were once underground can now be seen at Combestone Tor, on Dartmoor in England. ▼

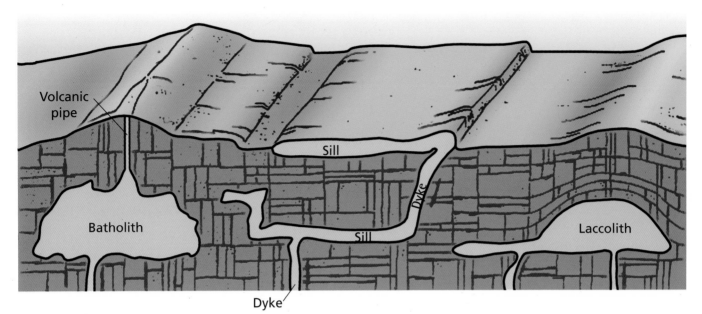

Laccoliths, dykes and sills

Laccoliths are made when the magma pushes layers of rock up into a dome shape. Dykes are made when the magma forces its way through layers of rock. When a dyke reaches the Earth's surface it is called a volcanic pipe. Sills are made when magma oozes between layers of rock.

Big Bend National Park

Big Bend National Park in the USA has some amazing igneous scenery. Volcanic activity between 25 and 70 million years ago left huge amounts of solid magma below the Earth's surface. The granite landforms can be seen as the rock above wears away.

▲ This diagram shows the different kinds of intrusive landform.

Mule Ears Peaks in Big Bend National Park are really two dykes running alongside each other. ▼

DID YOU KNOW?

Hekla's lava fields look like the Moon's surface. So American astronauts trained there.

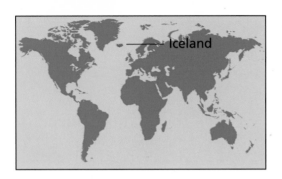

Iceland

In Iceland, new land is being created by volcanic activity. ▼

0 km   100

0 mile   60

Mid-Atlantic Ridge

Krafla caldera and power station

Lake Myvatn

ICELAND

Askja

Vatnajökull icecap

1996 eruption

Thingvellir   Geysir
                ●● Gullfoss
Reykjavik ●

Hekla

Heimaey
Westmann Islands
Surtsey   New volcanic zone

N

KEY

Belt of recent volcanic activity

Ice caps

Volcanoes

Iceland: a volcanic laboratory

Iceland is an island in the North Atlantic. It is above the meeting place of two continental plates, the Eurasian plate and the North American plate. New rock is made as the magma is pushed up between the plates. So Iceland is getting bigger.

Iceland is a young country because half its land area is less than 20 million years old. There are volcanoes, lava fields, hot springs and geysers everywhere. Lava fields cover 11 per cent of the land surface, and there are over 200 volcanoes. The most famous is Hekla which has erupted more than 20 times in the last hundred years.

In November 1996, there was a volcanic eruption under the Vatnajokull ice sheet. It caused huge floods.

New land

Geologists are very interested in Iceland. The most interesting place is a huge valley at Thingvellir in the area with the most active volcanoes. The new rock is slowly forcing the North American and Eurasian plates apart.

▲ An eruption in 1973 on the island of Heimaey, near Iceland.

Swimmers in the natural hot water of Iceland's Blue Lagoon. ▼

On 14 November 1963, the new island of Surtsey was formed. The crew on a small fishing boat saw clouds of black smoke rising from the sea near the coast of Iceland. The new island appeared within 24 hours. Today it covers an area of over 2.6 kilometres.

Ten years later, ash and cinders shot in the air from the volcano Helgafell on the nearby island of Heimaey. Lava flowed over the land and into the sea. It made the island bigger.

Although volcanic activity can be dangerous, it can also do good. Homes in Reykjavik are heated by power made from the hot springs.

Benefits of Volcanoes

Volcanoes can cause great damage to land and property when they erupt, and can kill people. But, despite this, more than 350 million people around the world live near active volcanoes. In Mexico, 30 million people live close to Popocatépetl. In Italy, 1.5 million people live on the slopes of Mount Vesuvius. Why do people take such a risk? It is because there are benefits to be had from volcanic activity.

Rice grows on the rich volcanic soil of Luzon in the Philippines. ▼

Fertile farmland

The lava that pours out during volcanic eruptions breaks down slowly over thousands of years to form very fertile soil. This is very good for farming. In Hawaii, volcanic soil is used to grow pineapples and sugar cane. Rice grows well in Indonesia close to volcanoes. And olives, vines, nuts, oranges and lemons all grow very well on the land around Mount Vesuvius.

A geothermal power station at Taupo in New Zealand. ▼

Volcanic products

When a volcano erupts, ash falls over a great area. At first this is bad for the land. But over the years, the ash slowly releases nutrients into the soil. When this mixes with water, the land becomes more fertile.

The products of volcanoes can be useful in other ways, too. Hot magma turns underground water into steam. The steam can be made into electricity in power stations. This is called goethermal energy. It is very important in Japan, the Philippines, Indonesia and Italy. Metals like copper, lead, zinc and silicon are found deep in volcanic rocks. Diamonds and opals are often found in the igneous rock made by volcanoes.

Predicting Eruptions

Scientists now know a great deal about how volcanoes erupt. They believe volcanic eruptions might fit a pattern of activity above and below the surface of the Earth. But they are still trying to find ways to warn people about volcanic eruptions before they happen.

▲ This scientist is measuring a bulge that is growing in the side of a volcano. The bulge shows that magma is close to the surface.

Early warning signs

By studying many eruptions, scientists know that several changes happen just before a volcano erupts.

- Small earthquakes happen as magma rises inside the crust. Waves of energy from the earthquakes are measured on an instrument called a seismometer. When scientists compare seismometer recordings, they can see where the earthquakes started. This tells them how close the magma is to the surface.

- The mix of gases in the air above the volcano may change as the magma reaches the surface.

- The volcano may change in shape as magma makes the sides bulge. Tiltmeters record even small changes in the shape of the volcano.

- When molten magma gets near the surface, it may raise the temperature of water above and below the ground.

To measure these changes, scientists have to watch volcanoes very carefully. The changes are often quite small, and can happen just before an eruption. Scientists use computer models to predict where the most severe effects might be. Then they can move people away from the most dangerous areas.

The ground moves as the magma rises. The tiltmeter records this movement.

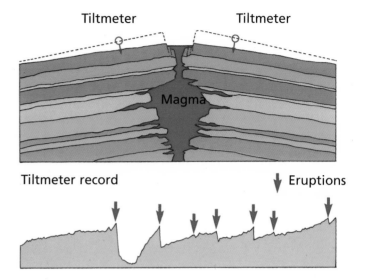

▲ Tiltmeters measure the tiny movements as the magma makes the side of the volcano bulge outwards.

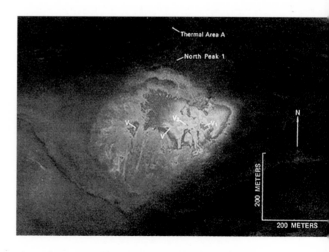

▲ This satellite picture of Mount St Helens was taken one month before it erupted in May 1980. The hottest part of the volcano is red.

Vulcanologists

The scientists who study volcanoes are called vulcanologists. They believe the best way to predict when a volcano is going to erupt is to study every new eruption when it happens.

Vulcanologists travel all over the world studying volcanoes while they are erupting. They need to protect themselves against the colossal heat from the volcanoes. They wear heat-resistant suits and asbestos gloves.

Many people have lost their lives near volcanoes. People who live nearby are often killed. Sometimes journalists and photographers who are reporting the eruption are killed.

▲ A vulcanologist in a protective suit, visor and gloves, in front of a lava flow.

LANDSBERG'S LAST FILM

Robert Landsberg was a photographer from Oregon in the USA. He made several visits to Mount St Helens in April and May 1980 before it erupted. On the morning of May 18, he was about 6 kilometres from Mount St Helens, his camera ready. As the mountain exploded, an ash cloud rolled towards him. He managed to take one last roll of film. It was found seventeen days later when his body was dug out of the ash.

Vulcanologists take these risks to try to save lives in other eruptions. Vesuvius in Italy is being very closely watched. Vulcanologists think a huge plug of solid rock may now be blocking the magma under the vent. This would cause tremendous pressure to build up.

Over a million people live in the city of Naples which is below Vesuvius. It will take a lot of time to evacuate so many people if the volcano threatens to erupt. That is why the scientists are watching it all the time. They can give warnings, but nothing can stop the volcano from exploding.

The next eruption of Mount Vesuvius could be a very big one. ▼

Glossary

active A volcano which still erupts from time to time.

atmosphere The gases surrounding the earth.

avalanche A huge fall of snow and ice, or rocks and debris down a mountain.

basalt Rock formed from thin, runny lava which flows quickly.

caldera The steep-sided crater formed on a volcano when the summit has fallen inwards.

core The centre of the Earth, below the crust and the mantle.

crater The hole at the top of a volcano.

crust The outer layer of the Earth.

dormant A volcano which is not erupting, but might in the future.

eruption What happens when magma from the mantle reaches the Earth's crust.

extinct A volcano that will not erupt again.

geologist A scientist who studies the structure of the earth.

geothermal energy Energy from the natural heat of rocks or hot springs in a volcanic area.

geyser A natural hot spring which sends jets of steam and water into the air.

hot spot The weak place in the earth's crust where magma rises to create volcanoes.

igneous Rocks made when molten material cools on the Earth's surface.

intrusive Rocks made when lava cools inside the Earth.

lahar A mudflow made when volcanic ash mixes with melting snow and ice or water.

lava The molten rock and liquid that flows from a volcano.

magma The molten rock in the mantle and core of the Earth.

mantle The thick layer of molten material below the Earth's crust.

molten Melted.

plate A large piece of the Earth's surface made up of land and seabed.

pumice A very light rock made when lava cools quickly.

pyroclastic flow A mixture of very hot ash, dust and gas that flows very quickly down the side of a volcano.

'Ring of Fire' The area round the Pacific Ocean where many of the world's volcanoes are found.

sulphur A yellow mineral that burns with a choking smell.

tephra Ash and dust from a volcano, carried along in the air.

tsunami A huge tidal wave caused by movements of the Earth's crust.

vent The pipe inside a volcano that the magma travels through before it reaches the Earth's surface.

vulcanologist A scientist who studies volcanoes.

Further Information

BOOKS

The Changing World: Earthquakes & Volcanoes edited by Steve Parker (Belitha, 1996)

DK Pockets: Volcanoes by John Farndon (Dorling Kindersley, 1998)

Focus on Disaster: Volcano by Fred Martin (Heinemann, 1996)

Restless Earth: Volcanoes & Earthquakes by Terry Jennings (Belitha, 1998)

CD-ROMS

Violent Earth (Wayland Multimedia, 1997)
PC and MAC versions available. Looks at earthquakes, floods, hurricanes, tornadoes and duststorms as well as volcanoes.

Interfact: Volcanoes (Two-Can, 1998)
Book and CD-ROM (dual-platform for PC and MAC). The CD-ROM includes interactive activities, puzzles and games.

WEBSITES

The World Wide Web has hundreds of sites about volcanoes. Here are two to start you off.

www.disasterrelief.org/
A web site which gives up-to-date facts about the latest disasters. The site is run by the American Red Cross, CNN Interactive and IBM.

http://volcano.und.nodak.edu/
Volcano World is a massive site that tells you almost everything about volcanoes. It has an 'Ask a Vulcanologist' feature to help you search through the hundreds of pages of the site.

Index